Our Changing Earth:
An Encyclopedia of Landforms

Darleen Ramos

Contents

Rigby
A Harcourt Achieve Imprint

www.Rigby.com
1-800-531-5015

Introduction

The land on Earth is always changing. Some of the changes are caused by the movement of rock deep inside the earth. Other changes occur when wind, rain, and ice move across the land. Let's look at some landforms found on Earth and explore what causes them.

Bay

A bay is an area of water that is almost completely surrounded by land. When sea or ocean waves crash against a shoreline for a very long time, they smooth away some of it and create a big curved area of water that we call a bay.

Because the water in bays is surrounded by land, there are usually no large and dangerous waves, even during storms. Sea travelers often sail into bays to stay safe when the weather is bad.

Canyon

A canyon is a deep, narrow valley with very high sides. Water forms a canyon as it moves through the bottom of the valley, wearing away the sides. It takes millions of years for a canyon to form this way. You can find rivers flowing through some canyons.

Did You Know?

- The Grand Canyon is the largest canyon in the world! It is almost 1 mile deep and 277 miles long.

- Native Americans lived in the Grand Canyon over 4,000 years ago.

Cave

A cave is a large, hollow area in the earth. Some are big enough for people to enter. We can find caves in the ground, on the sides of mountains, or under water. Caves form when water moves through tiny cracks in large rocks. After thousands of years, the water creates hollow areas in the rock. Large caves can even have lakes and rivers inside them from the remaining water.

popcorn pattern

straw pattern

Many caves have different patterns on the walls. These patterns form when water drips through the cracks in the rocks.

Did You Know?

Some caves have patterns on their walls that look like popcorn and straws!

Earthquake

There are many cracks in the earth's crust. The land holding these cracks together sometimes moves, causing the whole area of land around the cracks to shake. This shaking is called an earthquake.

Earthquakes can occur along cracks like this in the earth's crust.

10

When there is an earthquake, people can feel the ground shake and move under their feet. This shaking can knock down buildings and destroy bridges. A big earthquake can even change the direction of a river.

Did You Know?

In 1960 Chile had the largest earthquake in history, destroying the homes of 2 million people.

Glacier

A glacier is a very large piece of ice that moves slowly over land, like a huge, icy river. Glaciers form when falling snow does not melt. Slowly this snow turns into ice.

About 10,000 years ago, glaciers covered much of the earth. The glaciers finally melted, warmed by the hot sun. When they melted, they left many lakes and valleys. Glaciers also moved land and rocks from one place to another. Today we can still find glaciers in cold and snowy areas of the world, such as Antarctica.

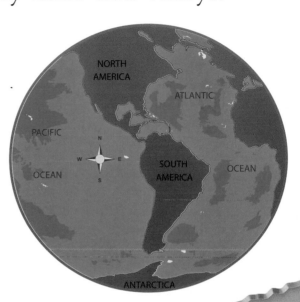

Did You Know?

Some glacier ice in Antarctica is almost 3 miles thick!

Island

An island is a piece of land that is completely surrounded by water. Some islands are millions of years old. Other islands are just forming. Some islands form when glacier ice melts, causing floods around the land. Other islands form when hot rock pushes through the ocean floor and then cools.

Today many islands are places to vacation and relax. Islands have also been places for sea travelers to rest and restock their ships.

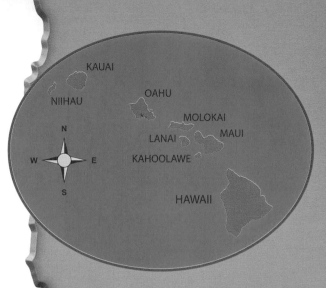

Did You Know?

The Hawaiian Islands stretch across more than 1,000 miles. This makes them the longest chain of islands in the world.

Mountain

A mountain is land that stands very tall and is steep and rocky. Some mountains can have rounded tops with a lot of trees, and other mountains can have rocky tops that are covered with ice and snow.

We find most mountains grouped together in mountain ranges. These groups of mountains formed millions of years ago.

This mountaintop is covered with trees.

Mountains form in many different ways. Older mountains formed when glacier ice melted long ago. The icy water moved rock to different areas, creating mounds of rock. Rain, snow, and wind continue to shape mountains that already exist.

This mountaintop is covered with snow.

Peninsula

The word peninsula means "almost island." A peninsula is a piece of land that is surrounded by water on three sides and connected to the mainland on one side. Some people think that peninsulas look like fingers!

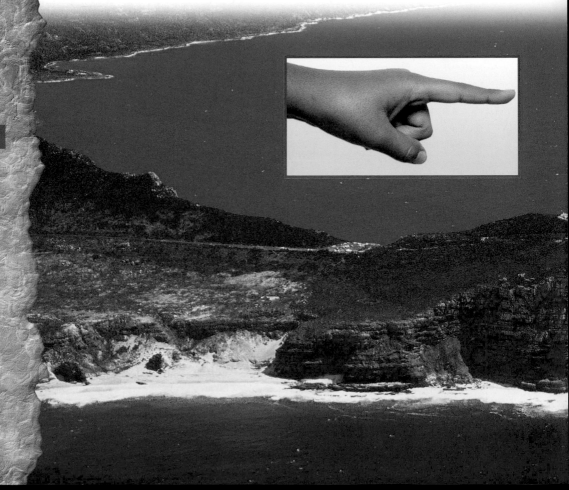

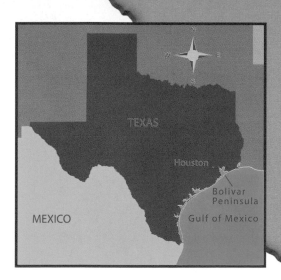

Did You Know?

Bolivar Peninsula near Houston, Texas, has many beaches and is 27 miles long.

Sand Dune

Sand dunes are piles of loose grains of sand that are built up by the wind. We find most sand dunes on deserts or near beaches.

Coastal Sand Dunes

Ocean waves and wind carry sand to the shore until a rock or a clump of grass stops it. A dune, or sand hill, will form where the tiny grains of sand fall.

Desert Sand Dunes

When wind blows loose sand in the desert, the sand piles up against rocks or bushes to form dunes. The desert wind can create sand dunes that are over 600 feet tall!

Volcano

A volcano is a mountain with an opening at the top. Rock deep in the earth under this mountain is very hot and is melted into a liquid called magma. Sometimes the magma shoots out of the opening at the top of the volcano. When the magma comes out, it is called lava.

Did You Know?

On May 18, 1980, the Mount St. Helens volcano in Washington had a very strong explosion that crushed trees 20 miles away.

Parts of a Volcano

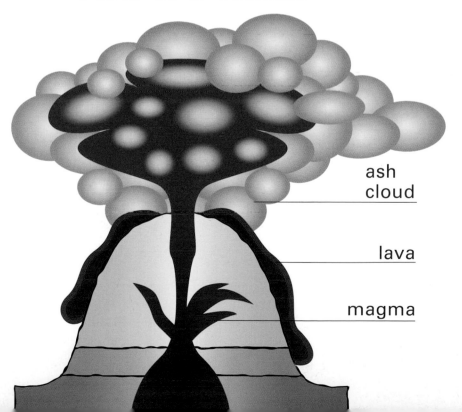

ash
cloud

lava

magma

Conclusion

Powerful forces above and below the earth's surface reshape our land every day. Even though some landforms take millions of years to form, others happen suddenly, without warning. From the deepest canyons to the tallest mountains, different landforms are wonderful reminders that our planet is always changing.

Wind and water created this rocky arch in Utah.